UNDERSTANDING YOU

UNDERSTANDING BOUNDARIES

by Elizabeth Andrews

Cody Koala

An Imprint of Pop!
popbooksonline.com

abdobooks.com
Published by Pop!, a division of ABDO, PO Box 398166, Minneapolis, Minnesota 55439.

Printed in the United States of America, North Mankato, Minnesota

052022
092022

THIS BOOK CONTAINS RECYCLED MATERIALS

Cover Photo: Shutterstock Images
Interior Photos: Shutterstock Images

Editor: Grace Hansen
Series Designer: Victoria Bates

Library of Congress Control Number: 2021951865

Publisher's Cataloging-in-Publication Data

Names: Andrews, Elizabeth, author.
Title: Understanding boundaries / by Elizabeth Andrews
Description: Minneapolis, Minnesota : Pop, 2023 | Series: Understanding you | Includes online resources and index
Identifiers: ISBN 9781098242121 (lib. bdg.) | ISBN 9781644948484 (pbk.) | ISBN 9781098242824 (ebook)
Subjects: LCSH: Boundaries--Juvenile literature. | Personal space--Juvenile literature. | Autonomy--Juvenile literature. | Social interaction--Juvenile literature. | Interpersonal relations--Juvenile literature.
Classification: DDC 152.4--dc23

Hello! My name is

Cody Koala

Pop open this book and you'll find QR codes like this one, loaded with information, so you can learn even more!

Scan this code* and others like it while you read, or visit the website below to make this book pop.

popbooksonline.com/boundaries

*Scanning QR codes requires a web-enabled smart device with a QR code reader app and a camera.

Table of Contents

Chapter 1

What Is a Boundary?

A boundary is an emotional or physical **limit** a person sets for themselves. People should respect the boundaries set by others. You're in charge of creating your own boundaries.

Watch a video here!

Chapter 2

Physical Boundaries

Personal space is one boundary a person can set. It is a distance around someone's body that you shouldn't enter without asking. Closeness might make them feel trapped.

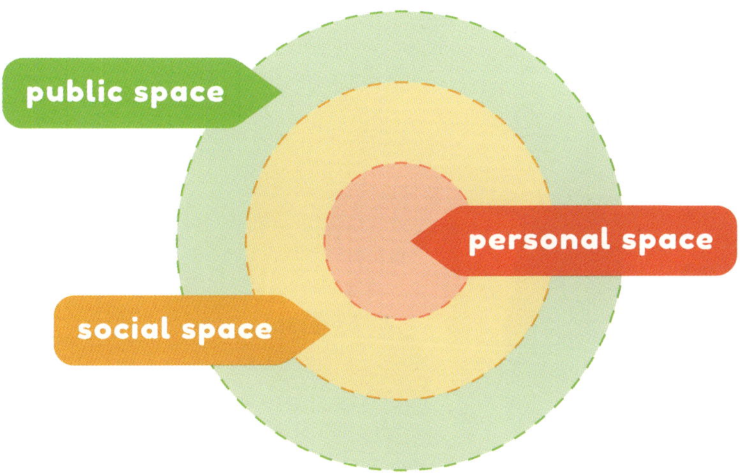

Learn more here!

E
M
D
S
YOU

Harry feels uncomfortable when his teacher kneels next to him at his desk. Harry asks his teacher to kneel in front of his desk instead. He is comfortable with that distance. His teacher respects that boundary.

Boundaries come from a person's wants, **values**, and feelings.

Chapter 3

Emotional Boundaries

People set emotional boundaries too. If a friend hurts your feelings, it is OK to share that with them. When they know how their actions or words made you feel, they can change them in the **future**.

Explore links here!

It is important to allow your friends to **express** how they feel about your words and actions too. Listen to what they have to say without interrupting them. When everyone has a voice, boundaries are easier to follow.

You can set a boundary by saying things like "please stop," "I don't like that," and "this makes me uncomfortable."

Boundaries are especially important when someone is going through something hard. Emma has a sick family member. Some days, she prefers not to talk about it. Her best friend Oscar always checks on her feelings.

If Emma says she is sad and tired, Oscar chooses to chat with her about happy things. He will talk about their favorite things, like soccer and art class.

Chapter 4

Respecting Boundaries

Respecting boundaries takes **empathy**. You must understand how others feel. Listen to what people tell you and trust that they know what is best for themselves.

Complete an activity here!

Setting boundaries might be hard for a person. They might feel like they are making life more difficult for those around them. But everyone deserves to feel comfortable and safe.

Making Connections

Text-to-Self

What are some boundaries you have set for yourself?

Text-to-Text

Have you read any other books that are about emotional and physical boundaries? What did they have in common with this one?

Text-to-World

How do you think people could respect their friends' boundaries better? Give a few examples.

Glossary

empathy – understanding and being sensitive to what other people are feeling.

express – to show.

future – what is going to happen.

limit – something that holds back.

value – something someone finds important.

Index

Online Resources

popbooksonline.com

Thanks for reading this Cody Koala book!

Scan this code* and others like it in this book, or visit the website below to make this book pop!

popbooksonline.com/boundaries

*Scanning QR codes requires a web-enabled smart device with a QR code reader app and a camera.